Hunger Fast

Cover design: Charlotte Chan/Popcorn Imagination
www.popcornimagination.co.uk
@popcorn_imagination

Printed in the UK
2022

ISBN 9798837685682

CONTENTS

INTRODUCTION

We all get hungry, it's a natural rhythm of life.

But we don't just want to eat anything; we want to enjoy it. We want it to be pleasing to the eye and made of wholesome and flavorsome ingredients that just pop when you eat them altogether.

Like that perfect brunch on a sunny morning, with a poached egg, lightly garnished with sprigs of watercress and chili flakes, that sings sweetly orange as the yolk runs down the avocado and sour bread toast

We want food that will fully satisfy our hunger and experience whilst nourishing our body in the right way.

However, there are times when hunger strikes, and we are unprepared.
For instance, when your stomach grumbles and cries out in hunger and there's no food in the cupboard or packed lunch prepared.

It’s not a good feeling and we end up in desperation mode. The only thought running through your mind is “where can I get some food, FAST!” And you end up grabbing the first thing you see, without any thought to its taste, enjoyment or nutritional value.

The feeling of hunger is a natural thing.

The body tells you it’s hungry because it’s getting to a point where it is low on energy and in need of a top up.
Hunger serves as a way of preserving your life, ensuring that you can run at the optimum level you need to function and live well.

Not only does it give you the energy for your day, but it actually increases your levels of happiness too. Just think of those moments where you sit at a table and you’re presented with your favourite meal, or eating warming food after a cold day outside. It's in those moments you feel the happiest and the hunger melts away.

It’s probably why we sit at a table together for meals, especially for group gatherings and birthday parties. We get to eat great food, have great conversations and remove our hunger collectively in togetherness and love.

Hunger is essential, but it is also a delight, and ensures that we enjoy eating a lot!

“What we hunger for most, we worship” - John Piper

As much as hunger is needed to maintain our natural bodies it is also essential to maintain our spiritual bodies.

When I think about it, I hunger for what makes me come alive. One of my steering verses is John 10:10.

“The thief comes only to steal and kill and destroy; I have come that they may have life, and have it to the full.”
John 10:10

To become fully alive, and fully who we were made to be, is the reason why Jesus came for us! To live life to the fullest with him.

But the question is, do we hunger for that? Or have we let our hunger drift into other things, things of this world, to satisfy the temporary “right now” stomach instead of our “eternal” self?

By focusing on the things of this world, we neglect our spiritual body and our muscles of faith waste away. Our mind starts to grow weary and confused because we’ve forgotten to feed our spiritual bodies. And we start to get headaches and feel faint because we haven’t drunk enough everlasting water from the fountain of life. We begin to forget who we were made to be.

The "food" of this world can take many forms. They aren't all bad, but if we hunger for these things more than God, we de-prioritise God. In doing so, we've given ourselves over to idols in our lives, simply because we've made them higher than God.

God knows that there will be times where we take our eye off the ball and forget to focus on Him. Just like when the Israelites were traipsing around the desert for 40 years. And yet God still turned up and fed them miracle manna bread and quail from the heavens.

God wants to restore you with his goodness. This book is an invitation to that. Come and eat with the Lord, sit awhile and rest awhile so that he can replenish you as you walk through your spiritual desert.

The Lord is with you, but you must choose a lifestyle that seeks to cultivate a spiritual appetite for the things of God.

1

TASTED GOODNESS

"Taste and see that the Lord is good.."

Psalm 34:8

When you taste something, you're trying it out for the first time.
And once you've tried something so delicious and excellent - you won't settle for anything less!

That's the same with Jesus.
I really enjoy going to food markets. It's that feeling when the place is buzzing with people and food vendors competing for your attention.
The road is filled with people walking up and down, eating and enjoying their latest food treats they've just purchased.
And without knowing it, they're acting as live advertising for the food stall, sharing to others the smells and looks of the food. Whilst everyone walks by secretly wondering where they got it from, looking everywhere to discover the answer they seek.

In the hubbub, street food vendors are out to engage you. They entice you over by offering you a taster or two of their best-selling food items on the menu, hoping that once you try it, you won't be able to resist buying it for yourself.

That is exactly what God is saying here in Psalm 34:8. Taste and see. Come over and taste God's goodness and all the good things that He can bring into your life. And He'll not just fill your plate for a moment, but for a lifetime!

The way we know Jesus and his goodness is by tasting it and experiencing it.

To have a personal encounter with the Lord is to experience him like no other. To sit at his table as a guest and feast on his goodness is what a loving relationship is truly like - not having to earn it, without any ulterior motives, but to just accept Him as He loves you. That is what it is to taste his goodness. And once you've tried it, you wouldn't want anything else.

"Like new-born babies, crave spiritual milk, so that by it you may grow up in your salvation, now that you have TASTED THAT THE LORD IS GOOD"
1 Peter 2:2-3

What I'm talking about here is God's presence.

We want our appetites to be for Jesus, because it's only Him that can truly satisfy us.

When a king enters a room, it's evident. The atmosphere of the room changes. You can almost feel the power, authority and superiority. You immediately feel the need to submit in awe and respect. There's a sudden hush that falls in the room in royal expectancy of what the king is about to say or do.

I was at a worship night recently where everyone else's agenda was cleared, so that we could enter into the presence of King Jesus. We surrendered to what he wanted to do, putting aside everything else, to worship and praise Him and Him alone.

It's all about the King. King Jesus, who is the Head of his Church.

"They have lost connection with the head, from when the whole body, supported and held together by its ligaments and sinews, grows as God causes it to grow."
Colossians 2:19

We need to reconnect with the King, removing all religious structures that get in the way of us drawing close to him. There doesn't need to be a barrier or a person we need to go through before we come to the Lord. No, Jesus removed all the barriers when he died on the Cross.

So come as you are and reconnect with Him.

God's presence is really what it is all about. Meeting face to face with the King, just as Moses did when he met with the Lord on the mountain. That one conversation made his face shine! It was the time he spent talking to God that set him apart.

Once you experience his presence, there's no doubt that he is real, there's no doubt about his love for you and what he can do through you.

There are many other ways that God's presence meets his people. I pray that you will encounter God in such a way that it is evident that he is alive and real in your life.

I encourage you to use this time now to spend time in God's presence. Invite him into this moment and become aware of Him. Because He never leaves us nor forsakes us. So therefore, His presence is always with us, we just need to be awakened to that and consciously spend time with Him.

2

EAT WITH THE KING

"...you may eat and drink at my table
in my kingdom..."

Luke 22:30

There was a King, who decided to prepare a great feast and invited many people to come and feast with him. When the feast was ready, he sent his servant out to tell the guests, but one by one they made their excuses. So, the king invited everyone on the street, the poor, the crippled, the blind and lame until his house was full.

This was a story that Jesus told in Luke 14:15-23.

The King is calling you to feast with him. Don't pass up on the opportunity to be filled and satisfied spiritually, the other distractions of the world are nothing in comparison.

God wants to prepare mighty awesome foods for you to eat daily, so that you will grow big and strong in his kingdom. He wants to eat with you, revealing with every mouthful, who he is to you and who you are to him. As we eat with the King, he shows us who we really are - seated in heavenly realms, children of royalty and our heavenly inheritance.

So how do we eat well and reconnect with the King? We must sit at his table and feast upon his goodness daily.

When Jonathan ate the honey, it brought revelation to his eyes about his father Saul. (1 Samuel 14:27)

In the same way, when we eat upon the food God serves up for us daily, more is revealed to us of the secrets and mysteries of God in our lives and what he is doing on the earth. And the best way is to take a massive bite of the Bible, his words.

"Man shall not live by bread alone, but on every word that comes from the MOUTH OF GOD."
Matthew 4:4

It's all based upon your diet.

So, if you feast on the things of this world, you will grow in the things of this world.
But if you feast on the things of heaven, you will grow in the ways and patterns of heaven.

"For the Kingdom of God is..righteousness, peace and joy in the Holy Spirit"

Romans 14:17

Everything we do flows from our spiritual practice and levels of spiritual health.

Do a spiritual health check up on your life right now. Are you eating the right things and how often are you eating from Heaven?

Things can easily be rectified. We just need to turn and fix our eyes back on Jesus. Draw back the dusty curtains, blow away the cobwebs and let the light shine in. Make space in your life for the rhythm of Heaven through worship, reading the word, prayer and fasting.

God invites everyone to eat with Him.

HUNGER.....

3

FASTING FOOD CREATES EVERLASTING FOOD

"Set your minds on things above,
not on earthly things."

Colossians 3:2

Fasting is when you give up something for the sake of pushing into something greater, so that you can become someone greater.

People fast many things, but mostly people fast from eating food. Fasting is like a spiritual detox. You deny your stomach food for the sake of cleaning out your soul, removing the junk of the world that your soul has been feeding on. This includes everything you've been listening to, watching and speaking about.

By fasting we spiritually reset our focus on God, re-calibrating our "stomachs", allowing heaven to determine our hunger.

Fasting accelerates our journey to hunger fast for God.

At the beginning of the year, our church fasted during January. It was a great way to start the year right and give God our first fruits.
It took a considerable amount of self-control, patience and a large dose of perseverance to give up my eating routines, only breaking my fast at 5.30pm. Each day felt like climbing a mountain of determination, choosing to power through the hunger pangs and deny my stomach. I had swapped my lunch and snacks throughout the day and filled up on God moments instead, choosing to speak with and hear from God.
As the days went by a new healthy routine kicked in, as I intentionally made time to dine with my King.

"Here I am! I stand at the door and knock. If anyone hears my voice and opens the door, I will come in and eat with the person, and they with me."
Revelation 3:20

You can think of fasting as a way of emptying the things and the loves of the world that we desire that actually block our connection and communication with God. And instead we allow for God to clean us out and pour the things He loves into us.

By fasting and temporarily giving up food, we are pressing into the eternal food of heaven. In doing so, God's word and His hunger for righteousness becomes our daily bread.

"Blessed are those who hunger and thirst for righteousness, for they will be filled."
Matthew 5:6

We begin to hunger and thirst for the things of God, for RIGHTEOUSNESS.

Righteousness is to be "Right with God" or to be "right standing in God".
This means that we live from a right relationship with God. In doing so we allow Him to shape our hearts and understanding of his good and perfect will for our lives. He puts us on a path marked out for our lives to travel with Him.

God calls us to be in relationship with Him, as it was always meant to be, when Adam and Eve walked with Him in the garden in the cool of the day. He's bringing us back to our first love. This has and always will be the right way to live our lives.

Just think of the closest person in your life right now. They're close to you because they know you, and how do they know you? Because they have cultivated a relationship with you, where you walk through life together, which has built understanding of each other's hearts and developed a depth of history and love.

In the same way, as we walk with the Lord, we begin to know His heart for us and others. It is when we grow in God's heart that we align with His will and values, changing us to be more like Him, righteous. And the more we become righteous, the more we hunger for righteousness, driving our transformation into being more like Christ.

I am so grateful that we can hunger for righteousness because of Jesus. Without Him, it would be unobtainable. Righteousness is only found in Jesus.

"It is because of him that you are in Christ Jesus, who has become for us wisdom from God - that is, OUR RIGHTEOUSNESS, HOLINESS AND REDEMPTION."
1 Corinthians 1:30

Fasting food is better than any fast food in this world. Fasting food satisfies the very depths of our soul.

4

FAST CONSECRATION

"Blow the trumpet in Zion,
declare a HOLY FAST.."

Joel 2:15

We fast to get right with God, to get holy, to be consecrated.

Wikipedia says that the word consecration actually means "association with the sacred". To consecrate something is to make something holy. When we fast we are in the process of making ourselves holy before God.

> "The root word of 'holy' means 'to cut' or 'to separate'. When applied to everything outside of God's, whatever is holy is whatever is SET APART unto and for God."[2]

So, in the same way that fasting consecrates us, it also sets us apart and makes us holy, just as God is. He is holy and set apart. By fasting we take a step closer to God and His holiness.

We become set apart from the world. In the same way that the Sabbath is set apart from any other normal weekday, it is made holy and special because it is outside of the norm. Heaven is also set apart from earth and any other earthly thing. Heaven operates outside the realms of our current existence here on earth and therefore is holy.

"Blow the trumpet in Zion, declare a HOLY FAST, call a SACRED ASSEMBLY.."
Joel 2:15

Fasting cleanses our appetite of the world, preparing us to absorb heaven into our spiritual diet instead.

The fear of the Lord leads us to holiness.

We fear the Lord in reverence of His awesome might, power and holiness. There is nothing and no one greater than him. It is that reason that we rightly fear, honour and respect God.
As we consecrate ourselves to God, we choose to be holy because He is holy.

You know that moment in the Jungle Book movie when the head monkey sings to Mowgli -

"Yooou ooh ooh I wanna be like you ooo oh, I wanna walk like you talk like you tooo ooo."

Well, that's exactly it!

We fast to know God in an intimate relationship with Him and to become something greater. To become like God, Christ-like. And this means laying down our desires and taking on God's heart. So that we become more concerned about what God wants and His kingdom. His kingdom which is based upon righteousness, peace and joy in the Holy Spirit. And we begin to walk a holy life, by applying his rhythms of prayer, fasting, reading his word and worship, into our lives.

"He has caused his wonders to be remembered; the Lord is gracious and compassionate.
HE PROVIDES FOOD FOR THOSE WHO FEAR HIM."
Psalm 111:4-5

5

FLAME-GRILLED OR SLOW-COOKED?

"...our God is a consuming fire."

Hebrews 12:29

Fire refines. Fire gets rid of any impurities in gold until it is of its purest form.
That is exactly what God does with us. He needs to clean us out of any impurities so that we will be able to fully carry His glory, His presence, His power and His authority. Without doing so, it would be like grabbing a dirty glass and filling it with clean water, and expecting it to be clean when you drink it.

God puts us through the fire in different seasons of our lives so that we become more refined. Flame-grilling us and spiritually making us more consecrated to Him in holiness. It's not an easy process, and everyone can testify that the shaking and removing of impurities in our lives is painful and requires us to face up to ourselves and our actions. But by the end of it, God dusts us off and polishes us up so that our true value and worth shines out. We become stronger and more dependent on God, trusting in His will and supply for our lives to bless others.

"Once more I will shake not only the earth but also the heavens....
Therefore, since we are receiving a kingdom that cannot be shaken, let us be thankful, and so worship God acceptably with reverence and awe, for our GOD IS A CONSUMING FIRE."
Hebrews 12:26-29

Oil is used a lot in cooking. Just go for a browse in the cooking oil section of the local supermarket and you will find all kinds of oils. They range from using oils taken from sunflowers, peanuts, walnuts etc. Each oil is fragrant in its own way and that gives it unique properties when cooking a meal. The best way to get oil out of a nut is to toast it on a hot pan. It's the interaction with the nut and the heat from the pan that causes it to release the precious oil contained within.

In a similar way, to release the oil and aroma from a lavender plant, it must undergo pressure and crushing. A process required to release the best of what was within it.

"For we are to God the pleasing aroma of Christ among those who are being saved and those who are perishing."
2 Corinthians 2:15

In the flame-grilling and the crushing and the pruning you are allowing God to clean you up and refine your character. All of which are important things, enabling you to carry the anointing oil and the responsibility required of you, for the next part of your wonderful life. But if He releases you too early, it will crush you under the weight of the power and responsibility, and so, we must go through the FULL process, without any short-cuts or power cuts.

It's a type of disciplining that we allow God to do in our lives, so that we can become more holy and righteous.

..."God disciplines us for our good, in order that we may share in his holiness. No discipline seems pleasant at the time, but painful. Later on, however, it produces a harvest of righteousness and peace for those who have been trained by it."
Hebrews 12:10-11

What happens if we choose to bypass the process?

Oil can only be achieved and refined in the process of heat, pressing or crushing. In the same ways anointing oil can only be bought through allowing ourselves to go through the same process spiritually.

In Matthew 25 there's the parable of the 10 virgins waiting for the bridegroom to let them into the wedding banquet. 5 of them were wise and brought extra oil for their lamps and 5 of them couldn't be bothered. But it was the 5 that brought extra oil who were prepared, who were able to be let into the wedding banquet when the bridegroom finally arrived. The other 5 were too busy trying to buy last minute oil that they missed their chance and weren't able to join the party.

This oil that the parable speaks about is anointing oil.

God anoints all of us to do his wonderful works on this earth. The word "anoint" in Greek even means to be consecrated and set apart. In fact, God marks us with the Holy Spirit, so that we belong to him in holiness.

"He anointed us, set his seal of ownership on us, and put his Spirit in our hearts as a deposit, guaranteeing what is to come."
2 Corinthians 1:21-22

It is the Holy Spirit that anoints us and provides us with the anointing oil to move in His power and authority, to keep our lights burning for Jesus and to carry out the purposes and plans He has for us and His church in the dark world that we live in.

So how do we continue to shine and burn our candles brightly? We must top up our oil through the Holy Spirit. It's like stopping at the local petrol station to fill up on more petrol, so that your car can continue driving to where it needs to go. Without the fuel stop, the fuel tank will eventually empty and the car will not be able to carry you to your intended destination.

It's the in-filling and dwelling of the Holy Spirit within us that enables us to carry out our calling and fulfil the destiny that God has placed in us.

Just as we discussed earlier, it's about spending time in the presence of the King, sitting and eating with him daily from his table. We operate from the secret place with God, in knowing the Holy Spirit, communing with the Father and walking with Jesus.

When you are passionate and hungry for more of him, you will willingly give and sacrifice all your time to God and want nothing else. You are willing to put yourself through the process because everything else in comparison is meaningless.

Wine must be trodden upon and squeezed out and then kept for years before its flavour is well developed and round-bodied enough to fully enjoy. Wheat must also go through a violent process of threshing and being hit multiple times with a rod and a sickle.

As we submit to God's discipline and spend valuable time with him buying anointing oil, the flavour of character within us is being built up and brewed to become a fuller and richer taste of Heaven. So, when the time is right and the wine is uncorked and finally opened and the flour is poured out to make bread - the quality and richness of your life will be tasted and admired, nourishing the whole body of Christ. And in that, the glory of God will be known.

Hold fast, this waiting time is not wasted.

The pain of your trials and tests have not been in vain. There is meaning behind the purpose.
And believe me, I know. I've had to restart in the eyes of the world, a few times over.
Throughout the years I've tried different jobs looking for the right fit for me and my abilities, and found myself travelling through various trials and challenges along the way.
And now, having heard from God, I'm pursuing a life as a prophetic artist and creative entrepreneur, at a time where everyone else around me is settling down, having families of their own and progressing up the career 'ladder'.

It's not easy, and at times feels like the wait is getting longer for other things in my life to connect up. But I believe that every step of the journey has been part of the process, where growth and maturity has taken place, increasing the value and worth of what I carry and create as a result. That wine within me has had time to mature and develop into a full-bodied flavour in Christ. I know myself more, and I know the goodness and faithfulness of God more, because I've pressed into the qualities and the voice of God through the low, vulnerable moments in my life.

Everything that is of real worth has to go under a process of refinement and sacrifice. We must go through the fire to come out better, stronger and closer to the Lord.

The way the process goes is different for each of us. But what can be expected is pitfalls and unexpected turns and sometimes falling flat on our face, I know, not an appealing thing. But, "it's not about the destination but the journey".

This process can be mirrored in food too. The longer we cure meat the more the flavours are expressed in a good slice of prosciutto. The same can be said with a good slow-cooked pork. In fact, the more processes the meat undergoes, the tastier and more flavoursome it becomes.

The meat must go through a process of tenderisation. It takes time, sitting to rest in salt, to break down the proteins. Then it's slow boiled in a gentle bath to wash off the salt and make it even softer, before being placed in the oven on a low heat, to further sweat it out and slow cook, allowing the seasoning to seep in and enhance the whole taste experience. All this is done to increase the depth of flavour of the mouth-watering pork pulled across a fresh ciabatta with a dollop of bbq sauce. Magnificent!

A slow process makes us uncomfortable. Living in a culture where everything around us is getting faster. Even the food delivery methods are getting faster and faster.

The idea of slowing down doesn't sit so well with the world. But God is calling us to rest. To rest and trust that his delivery methods are way better than any other.

> "Do not be afraid. Stand firm and you will see the deliverance the Lord will bring you today...The Lord will fight for you; you need only to be still."
> Exodus 14:13-14

But God is in the business of working on our character and enlarging our hearts, which is vital if he is to pour in and entrust us with the ability to wield his power and authority.

In the waiting, we must go through training, to prepare for when the time comes when God tells us that the time is right.

Like Mulan, we must tirelessly train day after day after day. So that in the pain and hard grafting, her muscles builds, her resolve strengthens, her determination and discipline become unwavering until she is fully prepared and ready for the battle that is up ahead.

This is what we must go through spiritually too with God, and the way he prepares us is through trials, through the fire, through the fast and the hunger and the testimony.

HOLD FAST

6

SALTED WITH FIRE

"Everyone will be salted with fire.
Salt is good, but if it loses its saltiness, how can you make it salty again?.."
Mark 9:49-50

We must go through the fire and into the salt to come out with the maturity and body of flavour. The flavour that we're looking to bring here is Christ himself, the tastes of Heaven and all the treasures that he brings.

The Chinese love to eat salty-eggs. It's basically duck eggs soaked in highly concentrated salty water for a good few months. And once ready, it's boiled and eaten with white rice and boiled green vegetables.

The creamy egg yolk takes on a flavour that is enhanced by the salt, making it tastier than usual, especially when you partner it with some plain white rice to balance it out.

The salt has the power to travel through an egg and alter it, completely transforming its taste and flavour! Applying the salt of God's word to our lives prepares and enhances our taste and flavour of Heaven.

God recognises that there is flavour in our lives, but it takes the salt, to activate it in us, drawing out who we really are in Him. Now, that's the flavour!

"You are the salt of the earth..."
Matthew 5: 13

I once discovered the smallest bottle of Tabasco sauce. It made me so excited to see it in such a miniature form. It looked exactly like the normal sized Tabasco bottle, with every detail. It had the same distinguished shape of the glass bottle, lid, label and logo too!

I stood there taking so many excited pictures of it, in between squeals of joy. The moment was further heightened when I turned the bottle around to discover the words "FLAVOUR YOUR WORLD"

To be Christians, we should carry the full flavour of Heaven on Earth.

We are miniature versions of Jesus, and contain the same powerful, flavourful kick of the Holy Spirit. And just like salt, chilli sauce is instantly recognisable, even when you add a single drop to the meal.

God calls us to be set apart and influence the world because of the potency of the Kingdom of Heaven that we carry.

This means that when you enter a room or even walk on the street, you bring the power and authority of heaven, your feet literally take the spiritual territory of the land. Demons flee and run away even when they see you a mile away. Your light and very presence clears the streets, the land, the buildings. That is what it means to be the salt of the earth and carry the flavour of Heaven. Because Jesus is in you, empowered by the Holy Spirit and covered by the Father's love.

Daniel was a guy who lived a life set apart and did so by choosing to eat differently. Instead of eating the luxurious food from the Kings royal table.

"But Daniel resolved not to defile himself with the royal food and wine, and he asked the chief official for permission not to defile himself in this way."
Daniel 1:8

Daniel and his friends chose to eat simply vegetables and water for 10 days. And after the 10 days they actually looked healthier and better nourished compared to the men who ate from the royal food. This is now known as the "Daniel fast".

This story goes to show that by choosing to eat the right things in God, we will be set apart and stand out from the crowd, the world and their ways. All for God's glory.

7

FIRE-FUELLED PASSION

"To have a passion for more of God is to be dangerous to the world.
– Charlotte Chan"

The more we hunger for God, the more on fire we become about God and His kingdom. The fire grows exponentially.

In the same way that we apply fire to a pan full of stock, we boil down its contents to create something full of concentrated potent flavour with the potential to knock out anyone with its strength of heaven's seasoning in every season.

God is all about FLAVOUR.

Daniel's friends Shadrach, Meshach and Abendnego felt the heat.

Their faith was tested, when they decided not to obey the King's command to bow down to a golden statue. They stood firm and did not waver in their resolve because they knew that God was greater than any king or idol.

So, they were chucked into a furnace that was turned up 7 times hotter than normal. But God protected them and even walked among them. The fire didn't burn them, in fact it PRESERVED THEM.

"They saw that the fire had not harmed their bodies, nor was a hair of their heads singed; their robes were not scorched, and there was no smell of fire on them."
Daniel 3:27

Passion is fire-fuelled.

And that means to do anything and go anywhere for Christ. To eat, sleep and breathe what God wants and says and does, living like Jesus so much so that when people see you, they see Jesus. You become transparently Jesus, living out what it means to abide in him.

"Remain in me, as I also remain in you."
John 15:4

Passion grows the more and more you experience the fire. And that fire is the fire of the Holy Spirit. The Holy Spirit is an all-consuming fire that burns up and reclaims the hearts of men that have grown tired of the ordinary. We seek to find the extraordinary in the biggest miracle worker around. Jesus Christ, raises people from the dead - reviving and restoring life into dry bones, giving sight to the blind and strength and hope to the weak. He is everything of excellence and grace and the greatest name above any other. Jehovah is His name; He is our saviour in every circumstance.

Since the beginning of time, man has always been fascinated by fire. Just imagine the cavemen dancing around the fire when the first fire was made with rocks clicking together over a small pile of sticks of their cave home. The joy they must have felt to feel that heat coming from it as the sun faded and the air cool settled around them. How their gazes were transfixed on the flames and how it sparked and danced in front of them as they stood and watched. Their experience of fire must have changed them, just its presence was powerful enough to mark them with awe and wonder.

The presence of the Holy Spirit changes us and makes us want to burn for Christ even more.

There was a song that I sang on repeat a few years ago, called 'Refiner"[3] by Maverick City, and it repeated this refrain.

"Clean my hands, purify my heart

I wanna burn for you, only you
Take my life as a sacrifice
I wanna burn for you, only for you"

Those words should not be sung lightly. They are the words of a person desperate for a move of God, passionate to see more of Him to be revealed in your life. That is what it means to burn for God. But as we know, it takes the refining process to make us holy and expand us, making space for more of God to consume our lives and radiate his light, flavour and aroma to the world around us.

Will Reagan wrote a song called 'Set a Fire[4]

"Set a fire down in my soul, that I can't contain, that I can't control. I want more of you, I want more of you God."

Now, those words are dangerous and should come with a fire warning!

Are you prepared for what will happen when you ask for a fire that you can't contain and you can't control? That is a bonfire explosion waiting to happen, and that's not something you can just assign to your Sunday morning worship service. This is a 24/7 furnace increasing in capacity that will erupt forth in your everyday. It will consume everything you have and blow like a mighty rushing wind, catching fire to everything and everyone in and around your life. It is a life that is sold out for Christ, where no cost and no distance is of concern to you. You burn uncontrollably for the things of God wherever you go.

The Holy Spirit, when given the space and permission to move in our lives, brings us completely in obedience to Him. This means that we give him the freedom to move us.

I remember singing the words of “Set a Fire” at the back of a church during a 24hr David’s Tent event. And it was like the Holy Spirit took me by those words and descended on me like a fire. Not just any fire, but a fire I couldn’t contain and a fire I couldn’t control. I felt the heat of the presence of God. My whole body began the shake and to sway like that of a flame. As the song increased in volume and tempo I began shaking, moving from bended position to standing position repeatedly, releasing a shout each time I did so. I literally became a Holy Spirit flame. I was burning for God.

There is nothing quite like experiencing the presence of the Holy Spirit. It’s exhilarating, like being shot with a billion bolts of lightning. With such a life power surge, you won’t be able to contain or control the body shakes and hand movements or the shouts and “WOAH!” moments in the Spirit.

To anyone watching, it is a little crazy. But when you understand that someone has given the Holy Spirit complete access and freedom to do what He wants to do in a life so passionate and sold-out for Christ. It begins to look like the most spiritually hungry person in the room!

FIRE
FALL

8

FIRE HUNGRY

Fire is fanned. An injection of oxygen to the flame is what causes the flame to grow.
Fire is therefore hungry for oxygen. Oxygen is what we need to breathe, our very breath of life.

When God created the heavens and the earth he breathed first, distributing his words that brought forth life. That very same breath of life fans the fire of the Holy Spirit.

A hunger for miracles, signs and wonders and to hear God's voice is what helped me grow.

In 2017 I went to travel Australia for a year, little did I know, God had other plans. I ended up spending the whole year in Perth, WA, walking with the Lord, and it was there that my flame was fanned.

Coming home I suddenly gained a new purpose, to seek out God wherever I went. No distance was too great, going all across London. I was so hungry to seek out God and learn to hear what He was saying and doing.

Lockdown was my Upper room experience. My hunger was set ablaze, as I sat at home eating and digesting teaching about how to hear from God and create with God. I was learning new ways to commune with God and develop an even closer relationship with Him - more than ever before.

I was burning to be even more on fire and passionate for the Lord.

I pushed more into the presence of God with prayer and petition - asking for God's mercies during the height of panic, when no one really knew what to think or do. It was during those encounters with the Lord in my studio, where I began to hear from Him prophetically about what he was doing on the earth right now. I received pictures to illustrate what God was saying and He would direct me to scripture to support what He was telling me. It was all so brand new to me and yet so exciting too!

When the disciples encountered Jesus, they knew immediately that there was something different about Him and gave up everything to hang out with Him and learn the mysteries that he carried. Every time they saw Jesus performing miracles, healing the sick and delivering people, I imagine that that would have increased their hunger for the miraculous.

And this is my hope for you. That by reading these words, they cause you to come alive and spark that flame of hunger for more of God in your life. You are made for more, and it is in partnership with the Holy Spirit that you will bear unusual and miraculous fruit.

A passion for God is powerfully explosive, and ten times greater than any atomic bomb ever made by man!

9

CLOTHED WITH POWER

"Everyone was filled with awe at the many wonders and signs performed by the apostles."
Acts 2:43

Once we are emptied of the world, made righteous and clean, then we are set ablaze with the fire of the Holy Spirit which cleanses us even further still. He increases our capacity and ignites us with His fiery passion, zeal and the power and authority of heaven!

The apostles were clothed in power on the day of Pentecost when the Holy Spirit descended upon them.

"When the day of Pentecost came, they were all together in one place. Suddenly a sound like the blowing of a violent wind came from heaven and filled the whole house where they were sitting. They saw what seemed to be tongues of fire that separated and came to rest on each of them. All of them were FILLED WITH THE HOLY SPIRIT and began to speak in other tongues as the Spirit enabled them."
Acts 2:1-4

Once Jesus died for us and paid the price for us, He ascended to Heaven and sent the Holy Spirit to fill and dwell in us, as a helper. After receiving Jesus in our lives, the Holy Spirit comes and dwells in us. Meaning that we become the place where the Holy Spirit can operate and bring God's presence.

This means that we are more than just ambassadors of Christ, because we are filled with His spirit, literally becoming a physical home for the Holy Spirit to live in, on earth. Allowing God to function and perform through us. In a way, he takes possession of us.
This means that we can operate prophetically when He moves and speaks through us.

I have felt the urgency of the Holy Spirit when he wants me to speak in tongues. It's so immediate that all I had to do was open my mouth and I would furiously speak in tongues, because the Holy Spirit needed to do something, and chose to use my mouth to do so.

This happened once when driving at night on a long road that drove right past Stonehenge. We were on the way to Wales, and the land was flat on either side of the road. We had no idea where exactly the stones were as it was pretty dark, just that they were there, marked out by the massive sign that said "Stonehenge". In that moment, the Holy Spirit kicked in with such an intense urgency in my spirit that I began speaking in tongues straight away, encouraging the others in the car to do the same. I have no idea what the Holy Spirit did, but I was obedient to his prompting and knew that I was doing his will.

The way that we get to that point is by making ourselves obedient and available for Him to move through us. We choose to live holy lives and righteous lives.

In doing so we sweep our house clean, kick out the skeletons from our closets, remove unforgiveness, hatred, anger, bitterness and unbelief. We make space in our internal house so that the Holy Spirit can take up residence in us, moving freely through His makeshift tabernacle within us.

Then we are ready to demonstrate the Spirit's power.

Paul writes:

> "My message and my preaching were not with wise and persuasive words, but with a demonstration of the Spirit's power, so that your faith might not rest of human wisdom, but on GOD'S POWER."
> 1 Corinthians 2:4-5

10

SPIRITUAL FULLNESS IN CHRIST

"..In Christ you have been brought to the fullness..."
Colossians 2:10

This is what it's about. Spiritual FULLNESS IN CHRIST.

God wants us to be fully satisfied with Him and Him alone.

He is calling us to sit, eat and feast at his table daily. To feast upon His goodness, His heavenly delights and to look upon his face. He wants us to feast to the point where we are so full that if someone offered us a snack, we would have to say “no”. There just wouldn’t be any space or appetite for anything else. Or anything less.

That is what it means to be fully satisfied with Christ. We don’t want anything else, but Jesus.

It is he who fills our stomachs, it is He who fills our every need and desire. Wholly Jesus, just Jesus, no one else will do. Just give me Jesus. No other junk food, no other substitution, just Jesus. We hunger for just Jesus.

“..In Christ you have been brought to the fullness...”
Colossians 2:10

When do we hunger for God most?

It is in desperation, in the desert dry and parched land. In the times where everything around you and your life is crumbling down to the ground. That is when we are most hungry for God. For God to come through for us, for God to bring the breakthrough and the miracles that we so desperately want to see. We cry out to God when we can't even see our horizon of hope to navigate our lives to His still small voice.

This is true of my life right now, as I write this. And so, it is funny that God should have me start to write a book on spiritual hunger even before I stepped into my most hungry and desperate moment of my life.

In Psalm 42 David writes in the middle of what seems to be one of his biggest battles and his soul is so downcast and saddened that he is needing to speak to it directly. And believe it or not, before I sat down to write this, I was in a moment of worship where I was shouting out loudly for the Lord to "restore my soul"

King David knew what it was to hunger desperately for the Lord. I think part of the reason was because he understood. He understood that it was about deep calling to deep.

"Deep calls to deep in the roar of your waterfalls; all your waves and breakers have swept over me. By day the Lord directs his love, at night his song is with me..."
Psalm 42:7-8

The reason why we hunger for more of God, is because we were created by Him, for Him. He is deep and so therefore we are deep. No matter how hard we try, if we are honest, we can't deny that it is Him that we desperately need to fill us, to complete us.

We may look to the world for temporary fixes - ice cream, pizza, chips, sex, drugs and rock and roll - but it never really satisfies. It never fills us up. You can't fill a need physically, when it's actually a spiritual need.

"You make known to me the path of life;
In your presence there is fullness of joy;
At your right hand are pleasures forevermore."
Psalm 16:11

We draw close to God from a place of desperation.

Fully aware that we are empty, there is no more spiritual juice left in the tank to keep us running forward. The car of our life has stalled by the roadside because there is no more fuel.

Our desperate hunger for God is what propels us into the deep with Him.

By hungering fast for God to fill us and fully satisfy us, we are becoming like the 5 wise virgins who over prepared themselves with more than enough oil. So that as the world gets darker, we will have enough fuel to keep our lamps burning and our light shining.

"I have told you these things, so that in me you may have peace. In this world you will have trouble. But take heart! I have overcome the world."
John 16:33

Desperation and hunger become the birthplace for revival.

Wildfires start in incredibly dry seasons where temperatures are extremely high. A simple spark can set off a wildfire running through dry forests, reaching speeds of up to 14 miles per hour.[5] Wildfires have been devastating in the past, eating and devouring everything in its way, simply because of desert-like conditions.

However, as much as the wildfire is devastating, it also benefits the ecosystem. It burns away decaying and diseased matter and plants and releases trapped nutrients in the soil.
Some trees, like the sequoia, actually rely on the fire for their seeds to open from the cones. Fire actually jumpstarts growth for the next generation of trees!

It is in the spiritual desert place where we find God to be more than we ever thought He would be. He provides that shelter for us when the sun is too hot and the road is scorched. When we become delirious and start to see double vision, He brings us to refreshing still waters, back to a place of clarity. Weary and tired we fall to the ground and the silhouette of Jesus bends down towards us and offers us His hand to help us up on our feet again. It is in the desert of desperation where we see that Jesus is our answer every time.

And just like the fire to the sequoia seeds, it opens us up and jump starts our accelerated spiritual growth, and hunger fans the flame. Now that the fire has burnt up the dead things in us and cleared up space, the new things God gives us can be planted and start to grow. Allowing God to grow and birth seeds of revival through us.

11

DIGEST FIRST THEN RUN

Once we gain the revelation that it is only God that can satisfy our spiritual hunger, we can't keep it to ourselves. We must share the food, the good food that is the good news.

First God feeds us and then we feed others.

In order for the gravy of revelation to soak into us and take full effect, we must give it time to absorb all the heavenly nutrients.

But sometimes the food may be so dense that we can't digest it. So, we need help to break it down before we can fully digest it.

Think of a baby chick hungry and squawking for food. Unable to catch fish for themselves, their parents must catch the fish and eat it first. When returning home their parents regurgitate up the fish for the baby chick to eat. The fish by now has been digested and broken down so that the chick can absorb it easily.
A lot of time when growing in hunger for God, we need to learn from those who have gone before us. Mothers and fathers in the faith that have walked with the Lord, who have taken the time to seek His face in the secret place and have received the revelation through the Holy Spirit and God's word. They are the friends of God. They are the workers in the field that have laboured over the land, turning it again and again until it becomes fertile. They've sown the seeds, watered it and watched it grow into a wheat field. They've gathered the wheat, harvested it all and milled it into flour ready to make and bake into bread. Only then, do they cut us a fresh slice of bread and present it to us with such joy, because their labour has borne fruit to build up the body of Christ.

Even as I sit here and write this book today, I am grateful for those that have gone before me, so that I may benefit from their bread- which has taken the form of books, sermons, movies and countless other creative ways. All of which has helped me on my Christian walk to digest and understand the ways of the Kingdom and how best to live a life that is pleasing and acceptable to the Lord.
And the process continues as we co-labour with God out on the fields, we bless the future generations in the same way.

I encourage you to get hungry and read books from other Christians alive and dead. Feed on their testimonies and lessons learnt on their journey through life with Christ. Share what you learn and inspire others to hunger for God.

12

HUNGER DAILY

"Our hunger for God matures our faith
and prepares our hearts for revival.
– Charlotte Chan"

Hunger reminds us to recharge, so that we can sustain ourselves. By hungering for God and constantly filling up on the things of God, we are sustaining and renewing the faith and hope within us.

As our appetite grows for God, we become bigger, better and stronger in our faith and our relationship with him.

Our muscles of faith build and bulk up, so that we are able to trust him with more of our lives. We become able to lift up weights that used to bring us down and step out and trust him in things that used to scare us.

We get to the point where, like Peter, we keep our eyes on Jesus and are willing to step out of the boat and walk on water. The miraculous becomes our everyday when we fix our eyes on God and run in a way that he has designed us to run. Each step becomes lighter because we are no longer running on earth but in heaven.

A heart that burns and hungers for God makes us ready to set others on fire for the Lord. It seeks for righteousness and justice which are the foundations of His throne. And because of this we stand firm as a representative of God. If anything inside or outside the church doesn't meet God's standard, then we must burn it down.

Yes, that can sound a little strange and extreme to many. But God wants to burn down processes and structures within the church, as much as outside the church. We are human after all, and in our humanness, we have allowed things of the world to seep into the Church. The world has contaminated the church and God needs to clean it out.

God revealed this to me in the illustration of a bee. It began with a single bee emerging from the striker tape side of the matchbox. As he emerges, he carries a piece of the striker tape and a matchstick in his hands. Joining other bees with trumpets they travel over great lands and distances, until they come across a hive. And then the bee strikes the match and sets the hive on fire. All the bees inside are forced to escape and fly out, leaving the honey to melt away.

God is in the business of sending out his church. Moving them from a place of comfortability to the frontlines of the battle that is about to arise. He is sending his hungry ones, his on-fire ones, his remnant to awaken the rest of the church to the new reality of "God let your Kingdom come, your will be done as it is in Heaven". He is moving Church into the new as we cross over from Egypt to the Promised Land. But this transition will be the biggest ever in history and it will look chaotic and controversial, but it is God.

God wants us to partner with him in bringing his Kingdom here on earth.

The only way we can do this effectively is to live a life as a living sacrifice to the Lord. This means to fully clean up our act and spiritually allow the Holy Spirit to cleanse our house, our inner living, our thought life and all other junk that we've kept in the loft of our minds. In doing so, we can free up space to allow God to work, pour out and move us to do what he calls us to do.

This process is a daily thing. Cleansing ourselves daily with his blood as often as we shower, and nourish our spiritual bodies with his word as often as we eat. We must continually hunger for the things of God. Putting aside the consumerist lifestyle of this day and age.

The Lord's Prayer asks God to "give us our daily bread" for a reason.

So come to the Lord. Feast with Him and grow in hunger and love for Him. And He shall miraculously multiply your harvest greatly. Just give him your two fish and five loaves and watch as He feeds the five thousand with it!

We are what we eat. So, let's eat right. Let's Hunger fast.

NOTES

References:

1. Piper, John (2022) A Hunger for God, Crossway
2. Hill Perry, Jackie (2021) Holier Than Thou, p20-21
3. Maverick City, Chandler Moore and Steffany Gretzinger (2019) Refiner, Tribl, Atlanta, Georgia
4. United Pursuit Band, Will Reagan (2010) Set a Fire, Knoxville, Tennessee
5. Welters, Claire (2019) Climate 101: Wildfires, National Geographic, https://www.nationalgeographic.com/environment/article/wildfires

Printed in Great Britain
by Amazon

86597606R00041